MI FAMILIA CALACA

MY SKELETON FAMILY

CYNTHIA WEILL

PAPER MACHE BY
JESÚS CANSECO ZÁRATE

Hi, I'm Anita.
Let me introduce my family.
I'm the big sister.

....

Hola, soy Anita.
Les presento a mi familia.
Yo soy la hermana mayor.

My brother Miguel.
He's a brat.

....

Mi hermano Miguel.
Él es muy travieso.

Juanito is the baby.
He's so cute!

....

Juanito es el bebé.
¡Él es tan lindo!

Us kids.

Nosotros los niños.

My beautiful mother.

Mi hermosa mamá.

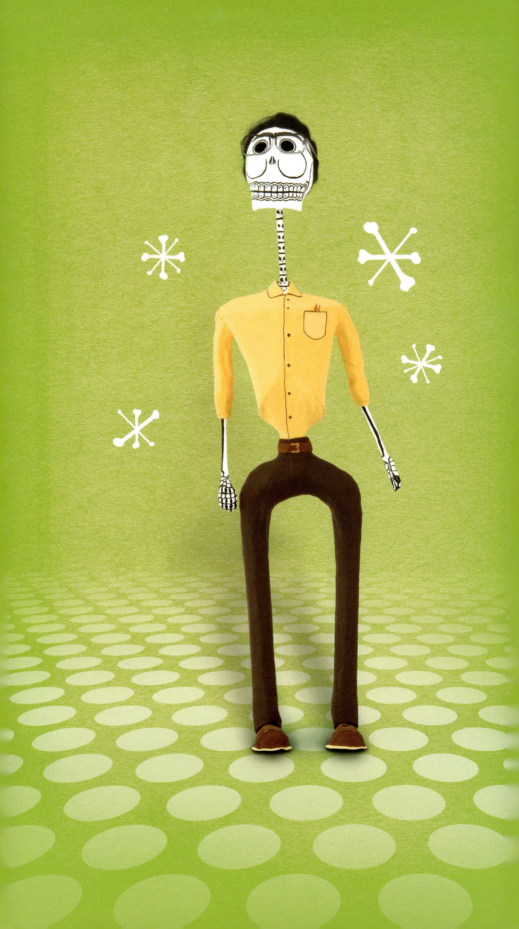

My handsome father.

Mi guapo papá.

My parents.
They are the greatest!

....

Mis papás.
¡Son fantásticos!

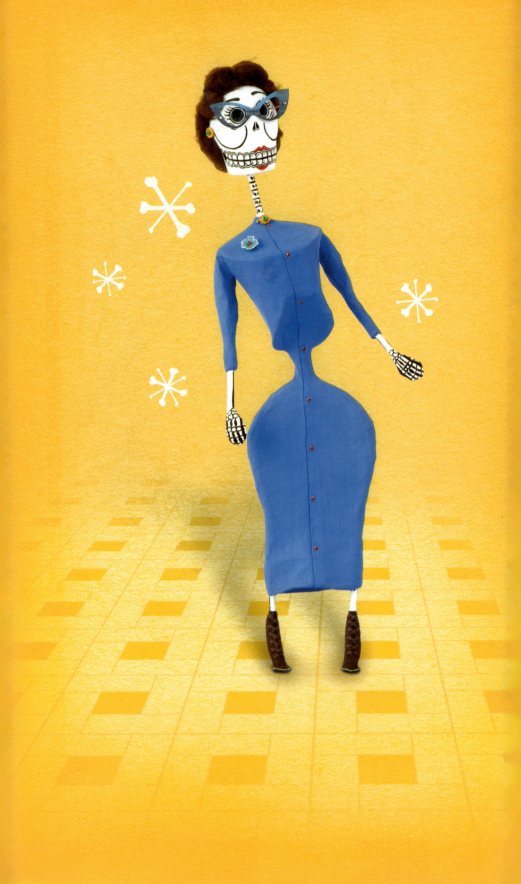

My grandmother.
She gives me good advice.

....

Mi abuelita.
Me da muy buenos consejos.

My grandfather.
He's so sweet.

Mi abuelito.
Él es tan tierno.

My grandparents.
They are the best.

....

Mis abuelitos.
Mis abuelos son los mejores.

My great-grandmother.
She tells wonderful stories.

Mi bisabuela.
Ella cuenta cuentos
maravillosos.

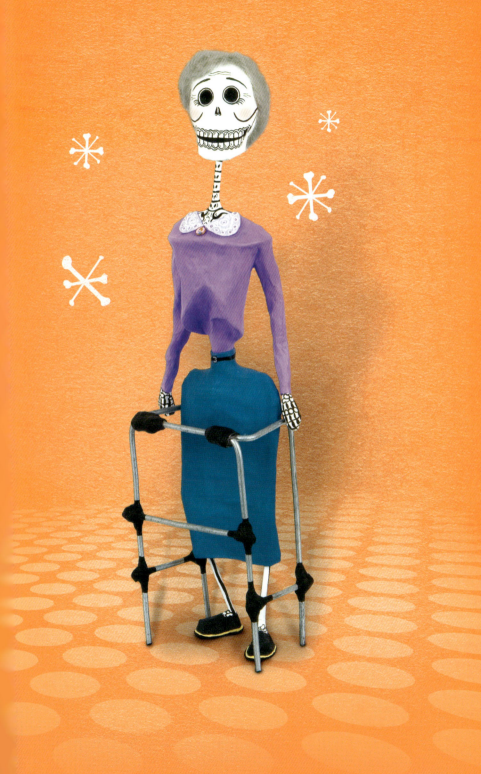

The pets.
My best friends!

Las mascotas.
¡Son mis mejores amigos!

The men of my family.

Los hombres de mi familia.

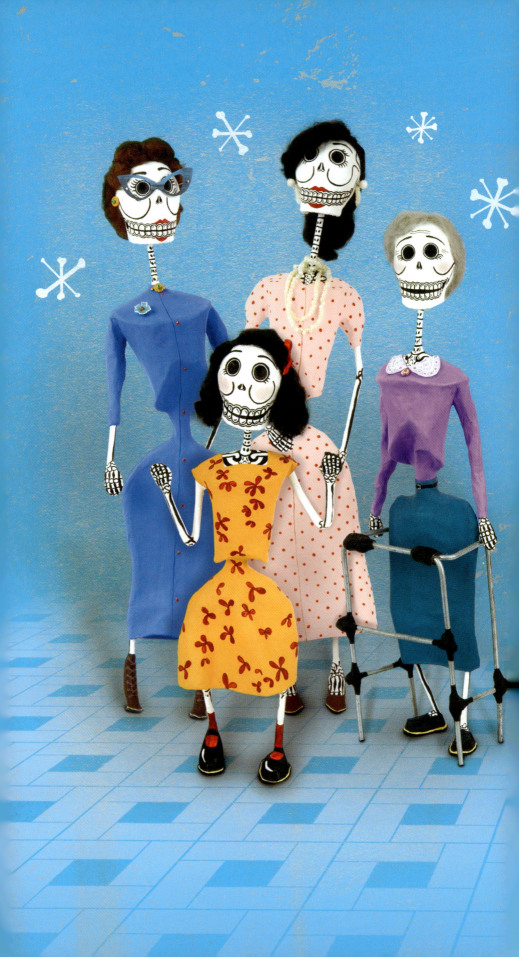

The women of my family.

....

Las mujeres de mi familia.

My wonderful family.
I love them a lot!

....

Mi maravillosa familia.
¡Quiero mucho a mi familia!

In Mexico the skeleton is a beloved and humorous figure. Its origins go back to pre-Columbian times.

To my dear friend Joyce Grossbard. This book would never have been made without your nurturing spirit and generosity.—Cindy

A mi madre Ana María Canseco que me ha apoyado y ha creído en mí y mis locuras.—Jesús

Photographer: David Hilbert

Thanks to: Stephanie Villarreal, Michael Donnelly, Jan Asikainen, Chloe Sayer, Olga Hubard, Christine Brown, Sarah Thompson, Emanuelle Guyon, Harry Baudouin, Ophelia and May Chapman, Nancy Mygatt, Ruth Borgma, Janet Glass, Anne Mayagoitia, Ruth Meyers, Vicky Weill, José Miguel Moracho, Bessy Reyna, Myriam Chapman, Museo Estatal de Arte Popular Oaxaca, Bank Street Writers Lab, and Friends of Oaxacan Folk Art.

Copyright © 2013 by Cynthia Weill. All rights reserved. No part of this book may be reproduced, transmitted, or stored in an information retrieval system in any form or by any means, electronic, mechanical, photocopying, recording, or otherwise, without written permission from the publisher. Cinco Puntos Press, an imprint of LEE & LOW BOOKS Inc., 95 Madison Avenue, New York, NY 10016, leeandlow.com

Manufactured in South Korea by Mirae-N
FIRST EDITION   10 9 8 7 6 5 4 3
Library of Congress Cataloging-in-Publication Data
Weill, Cynthia. Mi familia calaca = My skeleton family / by Cynthia Weill ; figures by Jesus Canseco Zarate. -- FIRST EDITION. pages cm
Summary: "Welcome to the Family! It's just like yours: father, mother, sister, brother, abuelita, gato. Well, but, there's something just a little bit different about this family. Maybe it's those clothes they wear...just a little bit fashion backward. And the colors! So vibrant and... lively. Maybe that's what it They are just so full of life. Familia-life from a Day of the Dead perspective!"—Provided by publisher English and Spanish. HC ISBN 978-1-93595-550-4   PB ISBN 978-1-94102-634-2   EBK ISBN 978-1-93595-551
1. Paper-mache sculpture—Mexico—Juvenile literature. 2. All Soul's Day in art—Juvenile literatur Families in art—Juvenile literature. I. Zárate, Jesús Canseco, illustrator. Sculpture. Selections. II. Tit Title: My skeleton family. NK8555.5.M64Z372 2013, 745.54'2—dc23
2013012342